Slimy Animals

Teddy Borth

Abdo
ANIMAL SKINS
Kids

abdopublishing.com

Published by Abdo Kids, a division of ABDO, PO Box 398166, Minneapolis, Minnesota 55439.
Copyright © 2017 by Abdo Consulting Group, Inc. International copyrights reserved in all countries.
No part of this book may be reproduced in any form without written permission from the publisher.

Printed in the United States of America, North Mankato, Minnesota.

052016

092016

THIS BOOK CONTAINS
RECYCLED MATERIALS

Photo Credits: AP Images, iStock, Shutterstock

Production Contributors: Teddy Borth, Jennie Forsberg, Grace Hansen

Design Contributors: Candice Keimig, Dorothy Toth

Cataloging-in-Publication Data

Names: Borth, Teddy, author.

Title: Slimy animals / by Teddy Borth.

Description: Minneapolis, MN : Abdo Kids, [2017] | Series: Animal skins |
    Includes bibliographical references and index.

Identifiers: LCCN 2015959002 | ISBN 9781680804959 (lib. bdg.) |
    ISBN 9781680805512 (ebook) | ISBN 9781680806076 (Read-to-me ebook)

Subjects: LCSH: Body Covering (Anatomy)--Juvenile literature. | Skin--Juvenile
    literature.

Classification: DDC 591.47--dc23

LC record available at http://lccn.loc.gov/2015959002

Table of Contents

Slimy Animals

Animals have skin!

There are many kinds.

Some are slimy.

They make slime!

snail

It feels wet. It can be smooth.

It can be sticky.

newt

It tastes bad. It can keep animals from being dinner.

slug

Octopuses use slime. It is **slick**.

It lets them fit in small spots.

octopus

Eels need it.

It helps them swim.

eel

Earthworms need it.

It helps them move.

earthworm

Slime can be bad.

It can make you sick!

salamander

Some frogs make it.

Bright colors say stay away!

poison dart frog

21

Other Slimy Animals

caecilian

sea hare

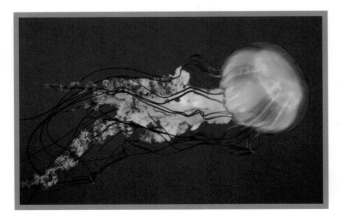

jellyfish

slime star

Glossary

bright
vivid and brilliant.

slick
smooth and glossy; slippery.

Index

abdokids.com

Use this code to log on to abdokids.com and access crafts, games, videos, and more!

Abdo Kids Code:
ASK4959

24